CANADA

Mt. Katahdin

VERMONT

MAINE

NEW
HAMPSHIRE

MASSACHUSETTS

NEW YORK

RHODE
ISLAND

CONNECTICUT

PENNSYLVANIA

NEW
JERSEY

OHIO

Emma Gatewood's
Farm

Gallia
County

WEST
VIRGINIA

MARYLAND

DELAWARE

WASHINGTON,
DC

APPALACHIAN MOUNTAINS

HIGAN

VIRGINIA

N

W   E

S

NORTH CAROLINA

APPALA

Springer
Mountain

GEORGIA

0   200

SCALE OF MILES

For Dad, who taught me
to keep going
—J.T.

The illustrations in this book were created using watercolor and
colored pencil on Fabriano hot press paper.

Cataloging-in-Publication Data has been applied for and may be obtained
from the Library of Congress.

ISBN 978-1-4197-2839-6

Text and illustrations copyright © 2018 Jennifer Thermes
Book design by Pamela Notarantonio

Printed and bound in China
10 9 8 7

Abrams Books for Young Readers are available at special discounts when purchased in quantity for
premiums and promotions as well as fundraising or educational use. Special editions can also be
created to specification. For details, contact specialsales@abramsbooks.com or the address below.

ABRAMS The Art of Books
195 Broadway, New York, NY 10007
abramsbooks.com

GRANDMA GATEWOOD

Hikes the Appalachian Trail

JENNIFER THERMES

Abrams Books for Young Readers • New York

Between eleven children, the clothes to wash, the cow to milk, the garden to tend, the occasional tramp passing through to feed, and one husband, Emma Gatewood rarely got a break. But, sometimes, she found a way to escape.

A long ramble through the hills behind the farm was all Emma needed to set her heart right again.

In the spring of 1955, when Emma was sixty-seven years old and her children had all grown up, she left her home in Ohio and set out to walk the Appalachian Trail.

Called the "longest footpath in the world," the trail stretched along the mountaintops from Georgia to Maine. Emma had read about it in a magazine. The magazine said no woman had ever hiked the entire length, and that it was easy. Besides, it was what she wanted to do.

Emma didn't tell her family where she was going, but no one worried. After years of hard work on the farm, they knew that Emma could take care of herself.

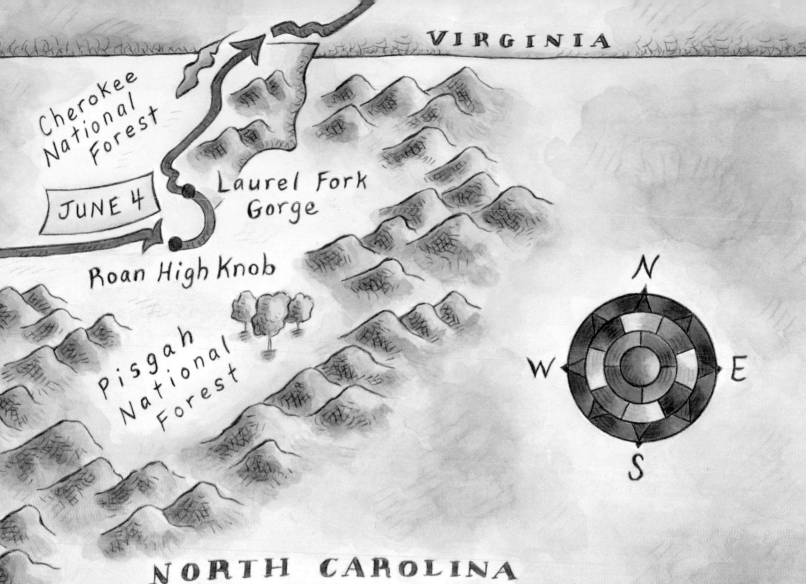

VIRGINIA

Cherokee National Forest

JUNE 4

Laurel Fork Gorge

Roan High Knob

Pisgah National Forest

N
W   E
S

NORTH CAROLINA

SOUTH CAROLINA

The Appalachian Trail is about 2,190 miles long, and passes through 14 states. It follows the chain of mountains known as the Appalachian Mountains, which are over 480 million years old. It takes about 5 million steps to walk the entire trail!

Emma wore canvas sneakers and carried a homemade sack, packed lightly. She ate berries from the side of the trail and drank from cold mountain springs. She rested under trees and on top of rocks warmed by a fire.

Some nights, the sky was so big and dark that Emma was afraid to sleep. Other nights, she curled up on a soft bed of leaves, with plenty of mice to keep her company.

Emma hoped to avoid meeting a bear . . .

. . . but she did, once, and chased him
off by hollering as loud as she could.

The trail ran over hills, across streams, alongside roads, and through small towns. At times, the woods felt like a long, green tunnel. Sometimes Emma lost her way, but even without a map, she always found it back again.

Some mountain farmers didn't know what to make of Emma,
with her hair like a wild woman after days and nights on the trail.
But most gave her supper and a cozy place to sleep. She often
found the kindliest welcome from the poorest of families.

Word traveled as she wound her way north, and Emma soon
became known as "Grandma" Gatewood.

VIRGINIA
WEST VIRGINIA

Harpers Ferry, West Virginia, is headquarters of the Appalachian Trail Conservancy. For this reason, it is called the "psychological midpoint" of the trail.

WEST VIRGINIA

Jefferson National Forest

JUNE 9

McAfee Knob

Black Horse Gap

ROANOKE

KENTUCKY

Burkes Garden

DAMASCUS

Mt. Rogers

Blue Ridge

NORTH

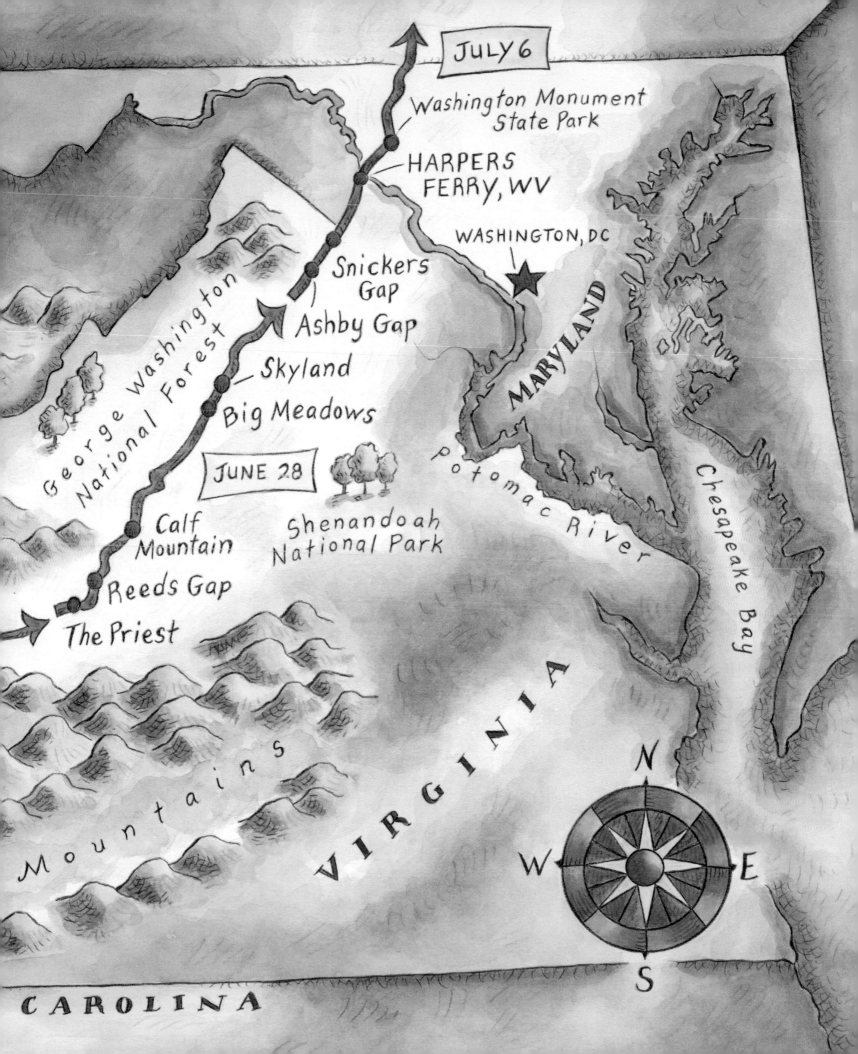

Emma scrambled up and down steep hills carved by glaciers that had melted millions of years ago. The trail wasn't quite as easy as that magazine article had said.

"For some fool reason they always lead you right up over the biggest rock to the top of the biggest mountain they can find," said Emma.

The weather turned from brisk and windy to hot and sticky—
and buggy!—to soaking wet to sunny, sometimes within a few
hours. But Emma kept walking.

Some days were rather dull. Other days . . .

. . . the views went on forever.

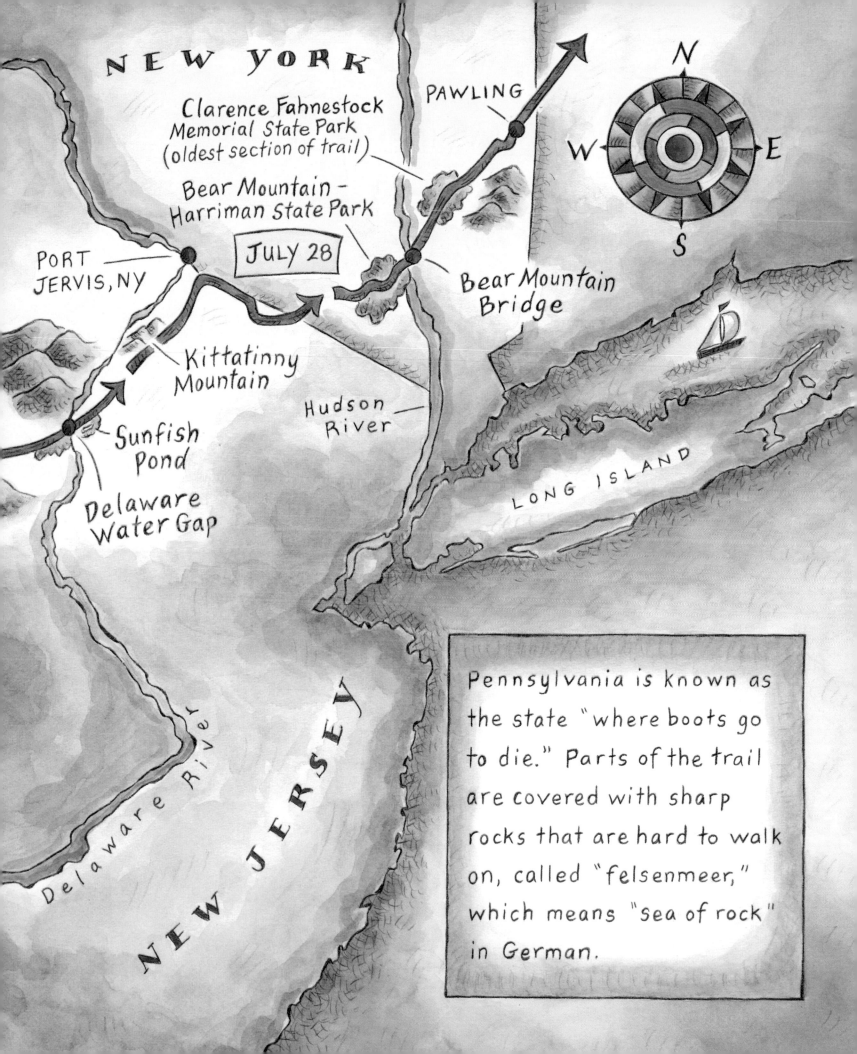

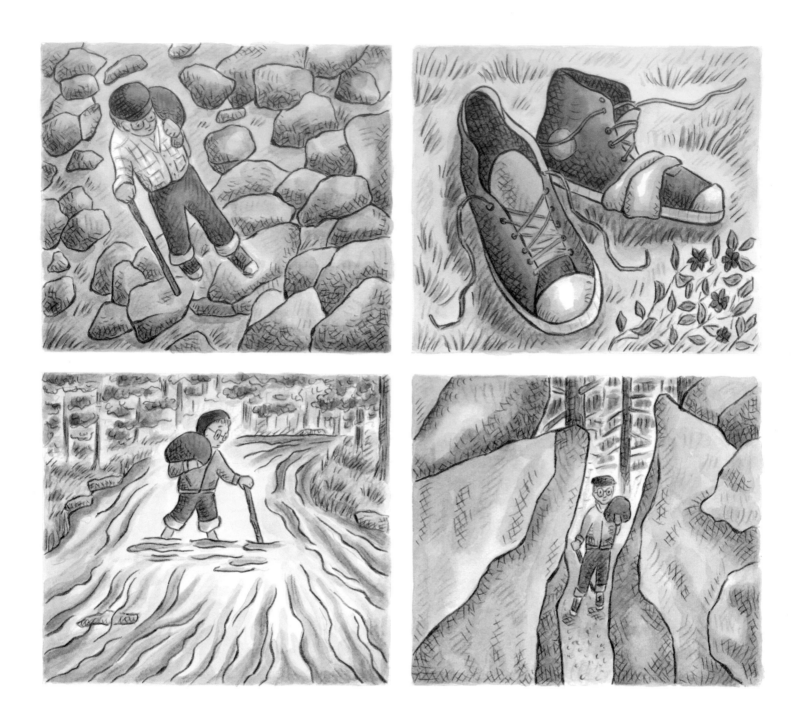

Rocks tore the soles of Emma's shoes, so she held them together with tape. She tried wearing a pair of men's leather boots, but they were big and clunky and slowed her down.

Emma chatted with everyone she met along the way, and when the newspapers heard about her big adventure, reporters met her at almost every stop.

Soon it seemed as if the whole country was curious about why an old lady would want to walk all that way by herself.

Emma answered, "Just for the heck of it." And she kept walking.

By late summer, Emma was over halfway
done with the trail. She had no idea that a
huge hurricane was racing up the East Coast.

The writer Herman Melville thought Mount Greylock looked like a great white whale in the wintertime. It inspired his famous novel *Moby-Dick*.

Kent Pond

WOODSTOCK

AUG. 20

Killington Peak

Clarendon Gorge

VERMONT

Stratton Mountain

Green Mountain National Forest

AUG. 11

Glastenbury Mountain

NORTH ADAMS

Mt. Greylock

PITTSFIELD

Berkshire Mountains

Housatonic River

Connecticut River

Beartown State Forest

Mt. Everett

SALISBURY

FALLS VILLAGE

CORNWALL BRIDGE

HARTFORD

AUG. 1

KENT

CONNECTICUT

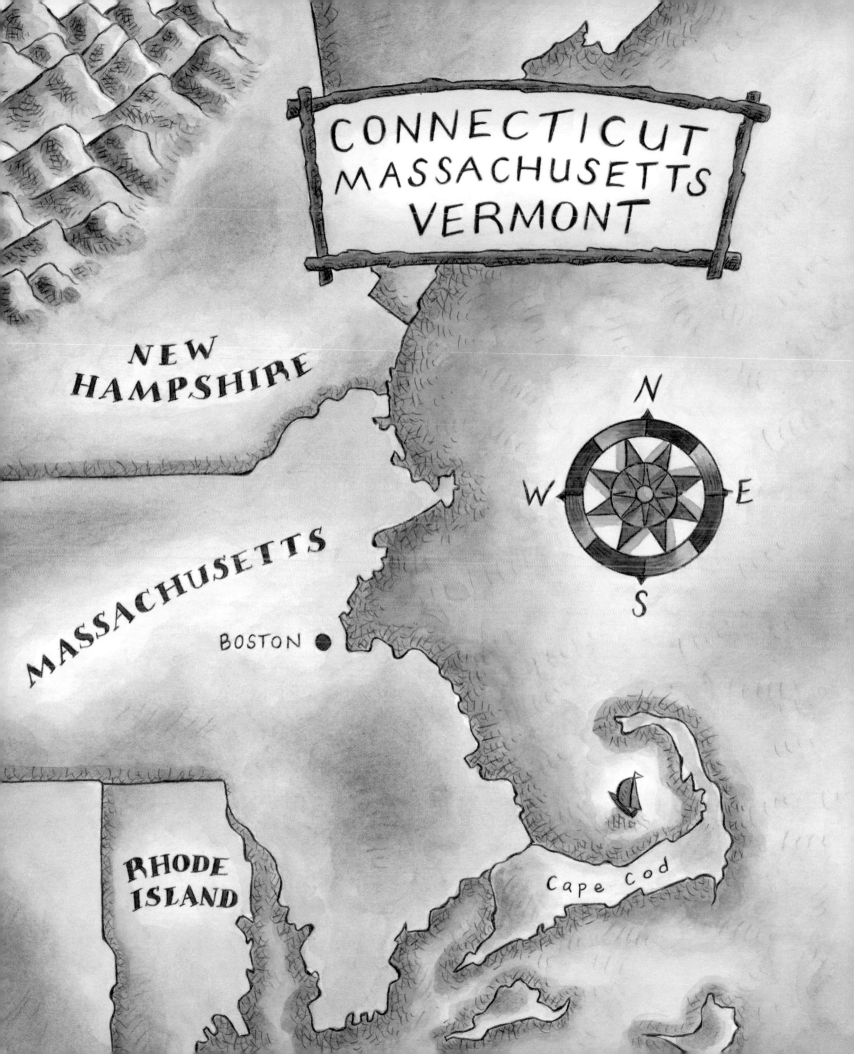

The storm hit hard. Rain soaked the land, and rivers washed away homes. Trees cracked in the wind, smashing to the ground. Emma didn't hear news of how much damage had been done, since she was deep in the forest. For her, it was just another day of foul weather.

She slipped on a ledge and twisted her knee, but kept slogging through the wet mud. She tried to cross a rain-swollen stream, but it was flowing too fast, and Emma couldn't swim.

Emma was tired.

She found a crowded shelter with a group of teenage boys from the city. The hut was tiny and damp, but Emma enjoyed their company, and they liked hearing her stories.

The next day, they carried her across the stream. She was on her way again.

Emma clung to two young men hiking together
across a swift-flowing river gorge.

She traveled a ways with a troop of Boy Scouts.

She was even invited to tea by a note that someone
had pinned to a tree. All along the trail, people
helped Emma. But after a while . . .

. . . she was glad to be alone again.

The second-fastest on-land wind speed ever was recorded in 1934 on Mount Washington, at 231 miles per hour. It broke the record books and the anemometer used to measure the wind.

Moosehead Lake

Kennebec River

Bald Mountain

CARATUNK

Mt. Bigelow

Rangeley Lake

Sugarloaf Mountain

CANADA

Saddleback Mountain

VERMONT

SEPT. 3

Bemis Mountain

Baldpate Mountain

Mt. Washington

Franconia Notch State Park

Mt. Lafayette

Goose Eye Mountain

Carter Dome

MAINE

Mt. Moosilauke

White Mountain National Forest

AUG. 22

Mt. Cube

PORTLAND

Moose Mountain

HANOVER

NEW HAMPSHIRE

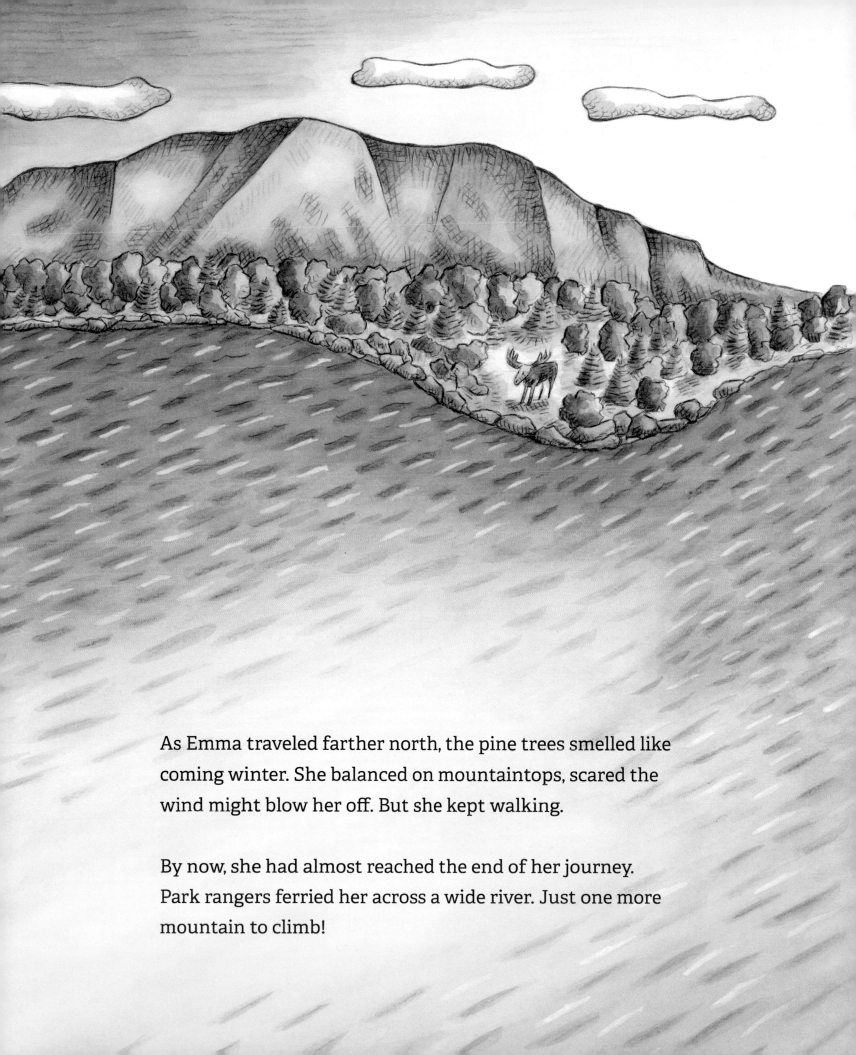

As Emma traveled farther north, the pine trees smelled like
coming winter. She balanced on mountaintops, scared the
wind might blow her off. But she kept walking.

By now, she had almost reached the end of her journey.
Park rangers ferried her across a wide river. Just one more
mountain to climb!

Emma wore every piece of clothing she carried, plus a coat someone had left behind on the trail. Her last pair of shoes was in tatters. It was bitterly cold. She could barely see through the thick fog and the eyeglasses she had cracked in a fall.

Her knees ached and her ankle was sprained, but Emma climbed, crawled, and pulled her way up the mountain . . .

until at last . . .

. . . she reached the top!

Emma sang a verse from "America the Beautiful" as loud as she could. She had set out to hike the entire trail by herself, and she did. Less than two years later, she would do it again.

"I wanted to see some of the things I missed the first time," said Emma.

NOTES

ABOUT EMMA

Emma "Grandma" Gatewood was the first woman to "thru-hike" the Appalachian Trail by herself in 1955, at the age of sixty-seven. A thru-hiker is someone who completes the trail from start to finish in one trip, while a section hiker does parts at a time, with breaks in between. She walked the trail again in the following years—the second time at age sixty-nine, and finally, in sections, when she was seventy-six years old.

Born on October 25, 1887, Emma married young and raised eleven children on the family farm in Gallia County, Ohio. It was not a happy marriage. After many years, Emma divorced her husband.

One day, while waiting in a doctor's office, Emma read about the Appalachian Trail in an old issue of *National Geographic* from 1949. The article made it sound like an easy walk, and since no woman had ever hiked the entire trail solo, she decided to give it a try.

Emma's first attempt at the trail was a failure. In 1954, she intended to walk from north to south, starting in Maine, but became hopelessly lost in the thick, dark woods. After breaking her glasses and wandering for days, Emma found her way back to a camp at Rainbow Lake. The forest rangers who had been searching for her said she was too old to be out there all alone. One year later, the same rangers would be shocked to meet her again, at the end of her successful trek.

At home in Ohio once more, Emma still wanted to hike the Appalachian Trail, but she knew that this time she needed to be better prepared. She went for longer walks to build up her strength. She saved her money and gathered her supplies. The next year, when spring came around, she was finally ready. Emma left home and took a plane, a bus, and a taxicab to what was the original southern terminus (ending point) of the trail at Mount Oglethorpe in Georgia. (It was moved to Springer Mountain, also in Georgia, in 1958.) Then, she started to walk.

Emma carried a few spare pieces of clothing, a blanket, and a plastic shower curtain for ground cover and protection from the rain. She packed a small first aid kit, some tins of chipped beef, bouillon cubes, and nuts and raisins. Her sack weighed less than twenty pounds. She trusted that people would help her along the way, and for the most part, they did, offering her home-cooked meals or a place to sleep—even if it was just a hayloft in a barn. Today, the idea of helping hikers is known as "trail magic." Kindhearted strangers leave packages of food and supplies along the route for any hiker who might need it.

The trail was harder than Emma expected. The hurricane of 1938 had blown down trees and damaged paths. With the advent of World War II, the country was focused on the war effort, and money to maintain the trail was scarce. By 1955, new highways crisscrossed the land. More people than ever owned cars, so they didn't walk as much as they once had. The trail had become overgrown and neglected and was difficult to find at times.

There were dangers as well—rattlesnakes, wild boars, and bears. Emma avoided sleeping in shelters as much as possible, since she was by herself and had to be wary of strangers. And though she had a few slips and falls along the way, she was never hurt badly enough to quit.

Emma walked twelve to sixteen miles a day—and sometimes more—and wore through five pairs of canvas sneakers. She changed from a skirt to trousers after brambles scratched her legs. Hurricane Connie hit the East Coast hard that year, but other than getting soaked, it didn't slow Emma down much. When she finished, after four and a half months of walking, Emma had lost thirty pounds, and her feet had grown larger by one size.

She became something of a celebrity. Local newspapers from towns along the trail wrote articles about her, and she was interviewed by a reporter from a brand-new magazine called *Sports Illustrated*. A few years later she even appeared on an episode of *You Bet Your Life*, a famous television show of the time. People were charmed by Emma's plainspoken wit.

Though no one really knows what drove Emma Gatewood to take on such a daunting challenge, walking inspires thinking, and perhaps it gave Emma time to reflect on her life. It also seems that Emma just really liked to walk. Besides walking the Appalachian Trail three separate times, she went on to hike the Long Trail in Vermont, the Buckeye Trail in her home state of Ohio (where a portion of the trail was later dedicated in her name), and the

Hawk Mtn. Sanctuary
PENNSYLVANIA

Delaware Water Gap
NEW JERSEY

Sunfish Pond
NEW JERSEY

Lemon Squeezer
NEW YORK

Bear Mtn. Bridge
NEW YORK

Mt. Greylock
MASSACHUSETTS

Laurel Fork Gorge
TENNESSEE

Charlies Bunion
NORTH CAROLINA

McAfee Knob
VIRGINIA

Shenandoah Nat'l Park
VIRGINIA

The Guillotine
VIRGINIA

Harpers Ferry
WEST VIRGINIA

Oregon Trail, as part of its 100-year anniversary celebration. Emma continued to push herself right up until she passed away in 1973, at eighty-five years old. Her determination inspired a renewed interest in being outdoors and appreciating nature, and in maintaining the Appalachian Trail for future generations.

ABOUT THE TRAIL

Benton MacKaye was a young architect and regional planner. In 1921, while sitting in a tree on Stratton Mountain in Vermont, he dreamed up the idea of a footpath that would run the length of the Appalachian Mountain range. It would link existing trails together from north to south and make it easy for people to take day trips and enjoy nature in their leisure time. MacKaye probably never imagined how many people would want to hike the entire length of the trail in one trip today.

Eventually a man named Myron Avery took over the physical construction of the trail with teams of volunteers. They chopped down trees, cleared brush, and marked new paths with white blazes painted on rocks and trees to show the way. They used a measuring wheel to track distances from one point to another, and built shelters made of logs and stones, located about one day's hike from each other. The first section of the trail opened in 1923 in New York, and the last part in Maine was finally completed in 1937. Though MacKaye intended for people to walk from north to south, most thru-hikers today travel south to north starting in early spring, to beat the worst of the summer heat in the southern states and the snow that can come early to New England.

In early days, much of the trail followed public roads and cut through private property, so the route was forced to change from year to year. But in 1968, Congress passed the National Trails Act, making the Appalachian Trail part of the National Park System and protecting it from development.

Today, the Appalachian Trail Conservancy (ATC) oversees the trail, with headquarters in Harpers Ferry, West Virginia. Local clubs in each state keep sections of the trail clear, and together they work to maintain and protect the thousands of species of wildflowers, trees, insects, and animals in the changing landscape.

NOTE: Some of the trail routes and place names are different today than when Emma hiked in 1955. Information on the maps in this book is from the current official Appalachian Trail Conservancy map published by the National Park Service. (An online version of the map is available at www.nps.gov/appa/planyourvisit/maps.htm.)

SELECT SOURCES

Andryszewski, Tricia. *Step-by-Step Along the Appalachian Trail.* Brookfield, CT: Twenty-First Century Books/Millbrook Press, 1998.

Appalachian Trail Conservancy. www.appalachiantrail.org

Appalachian Trail Museum. *The Early Days of the Appalachian Trail,* 2015; www.atmuseum.org/early-at-videos.html.

Brown, Andrew H. and Robert F. Sisson. "Skyline Trail from Maine to Georgia." Washington, DC: *National Geographic,* August 1949.

Browne, Robert A. *The Appalachian Trail: History, Humanity, and Ecology.* Stafford, VA: Northwoods Press, 1981.

Hare, James R. (ed.). *Hiking the Appalachian Trail,* vol. 1. Emmaus, PA: Rodale Press, 1975. (N.B. Quotes on cover, pages 9 and 43.)

King, Brian B. and Bill Bryson (foreword). *The Appalachian Trail: Celebrating America's Hiking Trail.* New York: Rizzoli, 2012.

Luxenberg, Larry. *Walking the Appalachian Trail.* Mechanicsburg, PA: Stackpole Books, 1994.

Montgomery, Ben. *Grandma Gatewood's Walk: The Inspiring Story of the Woman Who Saved the Appalachian Trail.* Chicago: Chicago Review Press, 2014. (N.B. Quotes pages 18 and 25.)

Shaffer, Earl V. *Walking With Spring: The First Solo Thru-Hike of the Legendary Appalachian Trail.* Harper's Ferry, WV: Appalachian Trail Conference, 1983 (facsimile ed.).

Clarendon Gorge
VERMONT

Mt. Washington
NEW HAMPSHIRE

Mahoosuc Notch
MAINE

100 Mile Wilderness
MAINE

Kennebec River
MAINE

Mt. Katahdin
MAINE

TIME LINE

1887—Emma (Caldwell) Gatewood born on October 25.

1920—Nineteenth Amendment is passed, giving women the right to vote.

1922—The *New-York Evening Post* runs an article titled "A Great Trail from Maine to Georgia."

1925—First meeting of the newly formed Appalachian Trail Conference in Washington, DC.

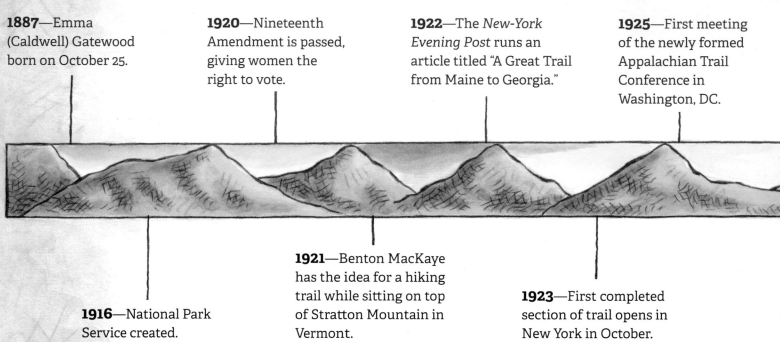

1916—National Park Service created.

1921—Benton MacKaye has the idea for a hiking trail while sitting on top of Stratton Mountain in Vermont.

1923—First completed section of trail opens in New York in October.

1941—Emma divorces her husband of thirty-five years.

1949—*National Geographic* publishes article about the Appalachian Trail. Emma reads it in a doctor's office waiting room.

1954—Emma's first failed attempt to hike north to south, before getting lost in the Maine woods.

1957—Emma hikes the trail for a second time.

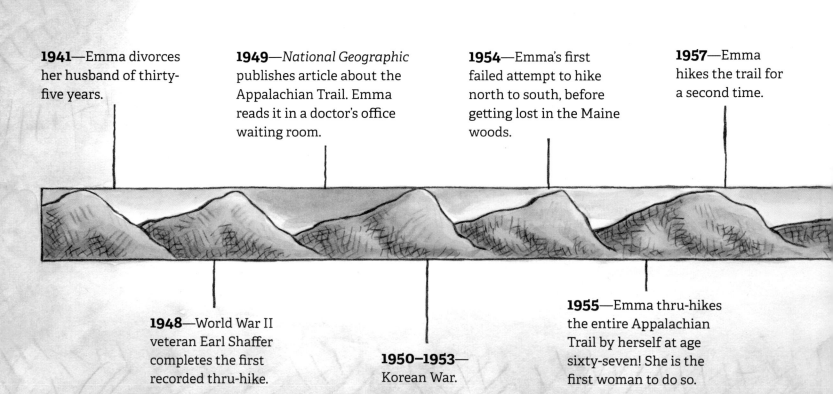

1948—World War II veteran Earl Shaffer completes the first recorded thru-hike.

1950–1953—Korean War.

1955—Emma thru-hikes the entire Appalachian Trail by herself at age sixty-seven! She is the first woman to do so.